Signs of the Times

compiled by Kenya Anders

©1999, 2010 By Kenya Anders

Published in affiliation with
David Anders Publishing House
A subsidiary of
Anders Peachtree City Properties, LLC
PO Box 2422
Peachtree City, GA 30269
E-mail us at: Signs@AndersUSA.com
Visit our website at: www.AndersUSA.com
Find us on Facebook at
David Anders Publishing House.

A portion of the earnings from every book sold by David Anders Publishing House goes to support underprivileged children in our community.
Find out more at www.AndersUSA.com.

ISBN-13:
978-0615455044 (David Anders Publishing House)

ISBN-10:
0615455042

All rights reserved. No part of these pages, either text or image may be used for any purpose other than personal use without prior written permission of the holder of the copyright or his legal representative. Therefore, reproduction, modification, storage in a retrieval system or retransmission, in any form or by any means, electronic, mechanical or otherwise, for reasons other than personal use, is strictly prohibited without prior written permission of the holder of the copyright or his legal representative.

Scriptures taken from the Holy Bible, New International Version®, NIV®. Copyright © 1973, 1978, 1984 by Biblica, Inc.™ Used by permission of Zondervan. All rights reserved worldwide. www.zondervan.com
Scripture quotations taken from the New American Standard Bible®, Copyright © 1960, 1962, 1963, 1968, 1971, 1972, 1973,
1975, 1977, 1995 by The Lockman Foundation
Used by permission. (www.Lockman.org)

To Rebekah, Lloyd, Luke, Rachel and Lincoln.

I have no greater joy than to hear that my children are walking in the truth.
III John 1:4 (NIV)

Table of Contents

INTRODUCTION 1
EPHESIANS 5:2 24
PROVERBS 4:27............................ 25
DEUTERONOMY 5:33 26
JAMES 1:19.............................27
JOHN 15:4 28
ROMANS 6:23............................ 29
PSALM 42:1 30
MATTHEW 22:37 31
PSALM 34:14............................ 32
GALATIANS 6:2 33
PROVERBS 14:12 34
JOHN 14:6 35
JOHN 3:30............................ 36
LUKE 21:33.............................37
PSALM 103:11............................ 38
COLOSSIANS 3:23 39
PROVERBS 14:11............................ 40
1 CORINTHIANS 10:13.............................41
ROMANS 8:37............................ 42
PROVERBS 22:6 43
PROVERBS 3:5............................ 44

MARK 10:15	45
PHILIPPIANS 4:6	46
COLOSSIANS 3:1,2	47
GALATIANS 2:20	48
EPHESIANS 6:14	49
PROVERBS 15:1	50
PSALM 91:1	51
DEUTERONOMY 5:32	52
1 PETER 5:10	53
HEBREWS 12:11	54
JEREMIAH 33:3	55
2 CORINTHIANS 12:9	56
EPHESIANS 6:16	57
PHILIPPIANS 4:19	58
LUKE 17:32	59
MATTHEW 7:17	60
PSALM 119:11	61
2 CORINTHIANS 5:7	62
1 CORINTHIANS 13:12	63
MATTHEW 19:5	64

Signs of the Times

merges God's Word with some familiar signs. These pages are intended for use during meditation and reflection at home.

Listen to God as He recalls these verses to your mind as you ride, walk, or drive around your city or town.

Please, however, give 100% of your attention to your driving when you are in the driver's seat. You have precious "cargo" on board!

―――

Kenya Anders

Introduction

I have hidden your word in my heart that I might not sin against you. Psalm 119:11 NIV

There is no greater authority, no better reason to explain the importance of teaching Bible verse memorization to our children than this verse, Psalm 119:11. We should all aspire to the command of Deuteronomy 11:18-21:

> *Fix these words of mine in your hearts and minds; tie them as symbols on your hands and bind them on your foreheads. Teach them to your children, talking about them when you sit at home and when you walk along the road, when you lie down and when you get up. Write them on the doorframes of your houses and on your gates, so that your days and the days of your children may be many in the land the LORD swore to give your ancestors, as many as the days that the heavens are above the earth. (NIV)*

In a world where our children's lives are already full of responsibilities and distractions — school work, sports teams, music lessons, video and computer games, to name but a few — the added goal of having our children memorize even one verse of Scripture may seem overwhelming. Enhancing this challenge is the fact that current educational curricula, at school *and* at church, have de-emphasized memorization of any passages of literature or the Bible. Future generations may wonder how well we served our children by not teaching them to strengthen their memory skills at an early age, particularly in regards to knowing Scripture.

I live in the real world, with five children, so I can already hear you putting up defenses and preparing excuses. I've used most of them myself! But wouldn't it be great if your child could learn five verses, ten verses, or perhaps recite the 23rd Psalm, the 100th Psalm, or maybe even the entire Christmas story in Luke 2? I believe most children can learn not just one of these passages, but all of them, and many more verses, not just because I'm an optimist, but because I've seen this happen time after time in children, not just my children, who were encouraged by parents and family members who thought memorization was important. Trust me when I say that your child could enter adulthood *"thoroughly equipped for every good work"* (II Timothy 3:17, NIV) with an armamentarium of 100, 200, 300 or more verses.

By now, Mommy (or Daddy) Guilt and frustration may have you throwing up your hands and shouting "How?" That's why I'm writing this book after more than twenty years of working with techniques to improve children's memorization skills and, equally important, incorporating that learning into everyday life situations. Before launching into the "Signs of the Times" portion, I want to provide some broader information on how to approach memorization with your children. Certainly not all of the tips will work for everyone in every situation, but I hope to provide you with enough ideas to get you started, and before long you will probably be adding more of your own.

As we start, realize that the ultimate goal is to instill Godly wisdom and knowledge into the heart of each child *"so that (they) may know Him better."* (Ephesians 1:17 NIV). Ultimately, memorization is just one of the many elements helpful in fortifying a relationship with God, and no specific number of verses is going to establish that relationship. Our children have a free will, so there can be no guarantee that memorization will keep them from straying, but retaining the Bible in their memory must certainly improve their odds for living a life pleasing to God.

In addition to the benefit of the opportunity to enhance their understanding of God, there is also a secondary benefit in memorization of Bible verses, which is the simple benefit of "learning how to learn." As I mentioned already, modern education theory has decided that children should not be required to develop their memories as was done in generations past. I do not understand how that approach improves our children's educations. As a college student, medical student and resident in Internal Medicine and then Dermatology, I was expected to master large volumes of information. This required many different memory techniques and skills, some of which had been honed as a child memorizing passages of literature and Bible verses. Most of my children have commented at some time to me that their school work was easier for them because of the different memory methods they transferred from having learned Bible verses.

You may argue that your child doesn't like to memorize. But how many of her favorite songs can she sing from memory? How many jingles from commercials on television or radio can your son sing along with, having memorized them all without even trying, simply because our minds are hardwired to hear and repeat? If you can create an environment that is conducive to learning, your children may amaze you.

So where do we begin? In childhood, of course – the earlier the better. A recent study showed that preschool children who were not yet reading already recognized the logos for McDonald's, Disney, Shell Oil, and even Toyota. Most children can't help but learn. It happens almost automatically. So let's provide them with something worth learning.

Think of a Bible verse you know and remember. If you are like most adults, you learned John 3:16 as a child. Several other verses may also come to mind, and most of them were also likely learned when you were still a child. Those verses we learn as a child have a greater chance of staying with us throughout our lives than the verses we memorize as adults. Not that adults should not try to memorize, but there is a greater retention in children – they can make it look so easy. Need more proof? Well let's look at what can happen when you challenge children to memorize, starting with the example inspired by Grandma Yates.

The last Christmas my husband's Grandma Yates celebrated here on earth, she recited the entire Christmas story from the second chapter of Luke in the King James version. Although she was over ninety years old, she repeated all 20 verses flawlessly, not because she had recently learned this passage, but because she had memorized these verses, and many others, when she was a child. The realization that her memory held onto the verses of her childhood throughout her long life further inspired me to want to foster that growth in my children.

Actually, she inspired me to want to encourage memorization in other children first. In 1989 David and I had been married for five years and were childless, but had six young nieces and nephews. As Christmas approached we went through the annual struggle with what gifts to give them. Their parents already provided them with more than they needed, and we wanted our gifts to have meaning. What would these children grow up recalling about the significance of the Christmases we spent together?

So we announced our plan to encourage Bible verse memorization and to do so to honor our parents by inviting all of their direct descendants to participate in a memory challenge. (Look for a copy of a recent announcement on our David Anders Publishing House website: **www.AndersUSA.com/Extras**). At our family Christmas celebration we would award one dollar for every Bible verse that any child could say.

You may protest that it is wrong to "bribe" a child into learning Bible verses. I would beg to differ with you. I prefer to adopt the Dave Ramsey method of teaching children a valuable financial lesson, that "work equals money". Do you offer inducements – financial, material, or simply verbal — to your child to do the things in life you deem important? My children's school has rewarded them with class pizza parties or tickets to Six Flags Over Georgia for achieving reading goals. Should Bible verses be any less important? We all respond to motivation. Our society encourages desirable activities (and sadly, some undesirable activities) with rewards to generate more of those activities. How we spend our money and assign awards reveals the value of those activities in our lives. Learning the Bible certainly deserves that stamp of approval. If you believe your child is not ready to be motivated by money, I am confident you can identify an appropriate inducement.

That first year of the contest our niece, Jennifer, was nine years old, and as the oldest in the group she led the way by quoting 14 verses with references entirely by memory. Her seven-year-old sister Laura said eight verses, and even three-year-old Jordan and two-year-old Nick got into the spirit with *"Jesus wept, John 11:35"* (KJV). A grand total of 24 verses were said that first year — a greater success than we had planned. We considered that $24 to be money well spent, an investment in their future. We were thrilled to hope that these verses could serve as the foundational verses in the lives of these children, knowing some of them would "stick" and last a lifetime.

We continued to reward children each Christmas and every year they rewarded us, adding to their repertoire of verses. At the age of 16 Jen did an astounding thing: she said over 100 verses, with a truly remarkable 133 verses that year! The second child to break 100 verses also did so that year, as Laura recited 107 at the age of 14.

But Jen and Laura were not the only children learning Scripture. Over the years our family has been growing — and growing and growing! David and I now have five children and 24 nieces and nephews. Eleven of that group have now moved into adulthood, and of that eleven, nine said 100 or more verses at least once (and most of them many times) before they "graduated" out of the contest the year they turned 19. Last year the group that is still young enough to participate said over 1,750 verses. Since 1989, 16 different children have said at least 100 bible verses in a single year, some before they were ten years old. Our niece, Lisa, said 398 complete verses *with references*, the year she turned 18. From those first twenty-four verses in 1989 to last Christmas 2010, our group has said almost 22,000 verses, complete, with references, and without cue cards! Want to see them in action? Go to our website at www.AndersUSA.com/Extras for a link that shows some of our family reciting the Christmas story from Luke.

From the onset we have wanted the emphasis to be the verses and their messages. So we have always offered "bonus" dollars for memorizing some select passages such as The Ten Commandments from Exodus, and of course, the Christmas story in Luke 2. A few years ago we fortified the value of Scripture with **"Legacy Verses"**. Each adult family member has been asked to submit the verse or passage of Scripture that has meant most to them in their lives. The children were offered an extra dollar for saying the Scripture if they could name the relative who claimed that "Legacy Verse". And they responded — many children could recite all 13 verses of I Corinthians 13 and say that it was the legacy passage for Aunt Buffie and Uncle Mark. Children ended different special verses with "Grandma Joan!", "Papa!", "Grandma Bec!", letting us hear they knew the importance of the selected verses for our family. Legacy verses bridge the generations, giving more identity to an uncle or aunt from another generation, and enhance the value of a verse by making it stand out from others because of its meaning to another family member. Uncle James Leitch was born in 1900 and has been dead for several years, but every year children still quote his verse and attach his name at the end: *"Thou wilt keep him in perfect peace whose mind is stayed on thee; because he trusteth in thee." Isaiah 26:3* (KJV) What a legacy!

The Memory Contest is just one way that you can

encourage your children to learn verses. While you may need to make changes to accommodate your family's situation, I am confident that you can. These awards have now extended beyond blessing just our family. A close family friend has adopted the idea for her grandchildren for over ten years. The teller at the bank (who helps David locate crisp new dollar bills or shiny golden dollar coins to award) now greets him after Christmas excitedly wanting to know how many verses were said that year. And a niece's school teacher has implemented memorization for her family, as I learned in an e-mail from my sister-in-law:

"... When she and her husband celebrated their anniversary this summer their family went to a cabin in the mountains. The gift she wanted from her children and grandchildren was for them to be able to share verses from memory when they were gathered together. On their second night together they had a circle time and gave each person a chance to say their memorized verses. She said that they had never done anything like that before and it was very moving and a wonderful gift to her... The "Legacy Verses" gave her the idea for her and her husband to share their favorite Scripture during the circle time... Today she stopped me and said to thank both of you for inspiring her. She said that good things continue to happen as a result of that night they shared—two of her grandchildren have felt called into mission work. God has worked in the marriage of one child. She wanted to make sure that she passed along to you her thanks for inspiring her. They will be rewarding dollars to their children and grandchildren for saying verses when they gather at Christmas. She can't wait!"

With stories like these, I am confident that you will be blessed by your decision to encourage Bible verse memorization in your children, grandchildren, or the children of others you love.

But how do you take the next step and get down to actual memorization? Are there ways to make memorization less repetitious and more enjoyable? Well, as best I can tell, yes and no. There is no getting around the fact that **repetition** is necessary to preserve a verse in our minds. But **association** is invaluable in making repletion more effective and more meaningful. We've all used association with various mnemonics to help us remember things. For instance, if you remember that the names of the five Great Lakes are represented by the mnemonic HOMES, you can more likely recall "Huron, Ontario, Michigan, Erie, and Superior". Associations trigger memories we have already stored quite effectively, voluntarily or involuntarily. When you go to the store and see a can of cheese dip it may remind you that you need a bag of chips. This involuntary act of association is nevertheless an effective memory trigger. We can all work to improve our recall of information by making specific associations much more frequently than we currently do. As you will see in the following section, the reason I wrote this book is to share the mnemonics I have created using traffic signs to stimulate memory and retention of Bible verses.

Certainly other associations can be helpful in the learning of verses. **Songs** are a great way to learn verses by association of words with music. Many of our traditional hymns are based on verses (for examples look in the back of your church hymnal or go on-line) as are contemporary praise songs. (Google is a great source here.) Specific tapes and DVD's have also been produced to let kids sing even more verses. Our family particularly loves the NIV Kids Club series (www.NIVkids.com) and we've effortlessly learned many verses from Proverbs, Colossians, and Psalms with this set of DVDs (although we started long before DVDs with VHS cassettes). Or make up your own song to be able to sing your favorite verses.

Body mechanics and **movement** can also help with memorization. Think of how many motions you know associated with songs such as "YMCA", "The Hokey Pokey", "The Macarena" or "The Itsy Bitsy Spider". Simple choreography can help children learn passages of Scripture. When helping my children learn the Christmas story in Luke 2, we developed a routine to show that

> *Joseph also went*
> *UP from Galilee,*
> *OUT of the city of Nazareth,*
> *INTO Judaea,*
> *UNTO the city of David, which is called Bethlehem; (because he was of the house and lineage of David:)* KJV

By pointing up, out, into, and unto, the children more easily mastered this order of the prepositions in this passage, and the rest more easily followed. Get creative with choreography, and with all associations, and you'll be surprised what your children (and you) start to retain.

Some associations may seem a little silly, but I've learned the sillier the better. When one of my children had a hard time associating the verse *"And my God will meet all your needs according to the riches of his glory in Christ Jesus"* (NIV) with its reference, Philippians 4:19, we decided a way to remember the association was that God would PHIL all our needs. And it worked!

If you have a creative active mind, you are probably a good excuse maker... even now you are saying, "OK, using associations might make memorizing easier, but I just don't have the time!" Maybe so, but I doubt it! Let me nudge you into looking into a few opportunities that arise during the day, and if you are honest with yourself you'll probably then find a few more unique to your situation.

Breakfast is a wonderful time to start the day off right. Instead of having morning drive-time news-talk radio blaring in the background with its unedifying reports of crimes and tragedies, why not play a CD of Bible verse songs. After just a few days your child will be singing along and in no time at all will likely know the entire CD, and you may pick up one or two along the way, also. Just don't be surprised if you find yourself humming your new tunes to yourself later in the day, even if you can't yet remember all the words!

Similarly, carpool and **chauffeuring** time is an excellent opportunity to play these CDs or to discuss other verses. Is it possible that what your children hear in the car right now is more helpful to their lives than Bible songs would be? This car time can be more valuable, even if you agree that you get to choose just the first fifteen minutes entertainment in the car. Believe it or not, even if they play a handheld video game or text their friends, they can't help but also be listening to what you select, so be bold!

Perhaps the best time for verses is at **bedtime.** My children seemed to have earned a graduate degree in the Art and Science of Not Going to Sleep. "Allowing" them to repeat verses to each other or listen to CDs once the lights were off seemed like a treat to them at times. As hall monitor during bedtime, I would oftentimes lead the way with other Bible verse games or quizzes, or simply reading passages of Scripture they were learning or reviewing. Verses can be selected to fortify what your children are learning at church, to help resolve problems they might be encountering, or to emphasize the particular season of Christmas or Easter. (Even the ones who pretend not to be listening or participating have shown the seeds are sown in their heart – soil doesn't have to want a seed to be planted for it to be planted!)

You can also **personalize** passages so they mean more for your child, making the Scriptures come alive. John 3:16 personalized becomes:

> *For God so loved Rebekah,*
> *that he gave his only begotten Son,*
> *that if Rebekah believeth in him,*
> *she should not perish,*
> *but have everlasting life.* (KJV altered)

Similarly, I would use all of the 139th Psalm to include all my children, cycling their names through as the passage allows. When doing so with my five children the first five verses become:

> *¹ You have searched Rebekah, LORD,*
> *and you know her.*
> *² You know when Lloyd sits and when he rises;*
> *you perceive his thoughts from afar.*
> *³ You discern Luke's going out and his lying down;*
> *you are familiar with all his ways.*
> *⁴ Before a word is on Rachel's tongue*
> *you, LORD, know it completely.*

> *5 You hem Lincoln in behind and before,
> and you lay your hand upon him.* (NIV altered)

Then close out your session with a 'Bedtime Benediction", a blessing over your children as they sleep. I particularly like Jude 24-25,

> *To him who is able to keep you from stumbling and to present you before his glorious presence without fault and with great joy— to the only God our Savior be glory, majesty, power and authority, through Jesus Christ our Lord, before all ages, now and forevermore! Amen."* (NIV)

What a wonderful way to take advantage of the natural tendency our brains have to playback and ruminate over the events of the day, especially the activities near bedtime, during the rest of the night as we dream and sleep.

Don't be surprised if you find you are spending more time in your Bible trying to get ahead of (or keep up with!) your children as they learn verses. You may want to organize a notebook, table, or spreadsheet to help your children see how many verses they've learned and to facilitate their review. Once again, you can't help but be the beneficiary of such time spent in preparation, being blessed by your children's efforts and enhancing your own Bible knowledge along the way. I have always been amazed each year as my sister-in-law, Janet, sits in to listen to her four children say their hundreds of verses. She's mentally clicking off each verse in her own mind as each child says his verses, and certainly has amassed a large mental picture of the contents of the Bible as she has helped her children prepare. As our own children, nieces and nephews have grown older they have created their own **notebooks** and lists to help them memorize more verses, and these notebooks, whether keep them or simply store them in their hearts and memories will hopefully guide them throughout their lives.

As the coordinator for your very young child's memorization program, you have the privilege of helping select which verses to choose to work on. Select passages that are interesting and meaningful for you, and research any words or concepts that seem foreign to you before teaching your child so you can fully explain the significance of the verse to your child. Choose verses that underscore a particular trait – patience, wisdom, kindness – you want your child to cultivate. Don't be surprised to find yourself reviewing verses on your own while you are washing dishes, commuting, or up late at night rocking a sick child. Take advantage of the opportunities as they present themselves in your real life.

Kill two birds with one stone – when I was a very busy medical student I loved to take time off from studying to go run. But even then while running I would take 3x5 cards and review the Bible verses I was learning at the time in a Sunday School class where the goal was to learn one verse per day. You have to carve out the time as it allows!

As you create associations or mnemonics, write them in the margins of your Bible so they will serve to trigger your memory the next time you read this verse. You'll be surprised how much easier those verses come back to mind once you see your notes.

So now you are ready to begin. You've selected the

verses you want to emphasize, you've gotten comfortable with understanding these verses, you've decided on which techniques and mnemonics to utilize in teaching these verses to your children, and you have even plotted out where in your daily schedule you will attempt to teach these verses. But how do you inspire your children to also participate? Without their interest, all your efforts may be in vain. So how can you keep learning stimulating?

The answer to this question lies in what motivates your child, and you are a far better authority on that than I. Nevertheless, here are some methods to try, and if you are like me you will likely stumble upon others that work even better in your specific set of circumstances. But in any case, distribute your praise and encouragement liberally. Repetition is an essential part of learning, so you must keep things light and positive. No one enjoys boring repetitive activities.

In no particular order, here are some of the methods I've employed to keep my children interested in learning verses. I've given the methods various names which the children know and recognize, with each child seeming to develop his own favorite style of "game" in making memory learning fun. Each method includes the children in an active fashion which helps to transfer it from "mine" to "theirs." These also help develop their ability to listen carefully, focus intently and cooperate as a team – which will help them in many areas of their development and education.

"Copy Cat" — This simply involves a "repeat after me" style of learning where I say part of the verse and then let the child repeat that portion back to me. As the child masters more verses, the child can become the leader (and believe me, they will!), getting you to echo back the verses as they say them first.

"Help!" — In this variation of verbal "fill in the blanks", I will say most of the verse, then let the child fill in a key word within the verse. Over time, I put more "blanks" in the verse, as the child becomes more and more familiar with the text — maybe even every other word. This teaches them to be accurate in their memorizing, which is important later in life. It seems it is our human nature to get sloppy over time with various repeated activities, but the "Help!" version requires accurate learning, thus delaying or averting any imprecision and teaching the skill of precision. (Do you want your brain surgeon "kind of sure" about what they are doing on you?) Once again, as the child masters the verse, he can assume the role of leader, and you might be surprised with how he will enjoy putting you on the spot to fill in a specific missing word.

"Duck Duck Goose" — This version works best with three or more participants. The leader goes around in an order – maybe by age, or seating order in the car, etc. – reciting a short phrase or a certain number of words, then moving to the next child (or participating parent or grandparent) to say the next phrase, and on reaching the third person, he or she contributes the next words or phrase, continuing around the circle ad lib.

"Tag, You're IT!" — Similar to "Duck, Duck, Goose", but in random order among all the participants. The leader stops at a random spot and calls out the person who will take over. The random order of selection will really keep everyone on his toes.

"Ping-Pong" or "Around the World" — Each participant contributes one word (or syllable!) in a rapid fire sequence, best played once a verse is fairly well known.

"Around the World" goes around a circle of participants, in order, and works well in a car. In "Ping-Pong" things really get interesting as the leader points randomly and rapidly at any participant.

"Robots" — In this version, a musical metronome is set at a slow speed (which can be accelerated with time and practice) and the speaker is encouraged to use a flat monotone robot voice to say one syllable per click of the metronome. This technique is helpful in establishing smoother word recall and can refresh verses already learned when words are getting sloppy.

I've also let my children **write** their verses quietly at times when they were getting restless during "big church". When they are younger, you might pass over a verse partially written and let them fill in the blanks. They are often very glad for the distraction and this keeps them focused on things of God.

For younger children we used a memory aid that we learned from David's sister, Janet, when her children were too young to read. (She adopted four precious children, three of whom arrived at the same time at 3, 13, and 27 months of age). On the highchair tray after meals different colors of M&M's are used to remind the child of specific Bible verses, and reward him for successfully repeating a verse. If your kids learn better tying verses to broccoli, carrots and asparagus, by all means use these rather than M&M's — either will sharpen the reflex associations. Pavlov's dogs weren't smarter than your kids!

These are just a few ways you can prevent monotony from setting in as your child uses techniques to leverage repetition into long-term memory.

Once you and your child have learned a verse, use it to bless yourself, each other, others you know, and to glorify God. You can bless yourself with verses learned anytime you have free time, planned or otherwise. Up in the middle of the night with a sick child? Fortify yourself with reminders of God's love. Unable to sleep? Rather than counting sheep, say your verses, to focus your mind on God and his promises, protection, and personality, rather than your problems. Waiting in carpool line for pick up? Review the verses you know.

Bless your children with what you have learned by assigning them their own legacy verses, based on the strength of character you want them obtain. Learn important snippets and then quote them at important times — you can go back and learn the entire verse when you want. On more than one occasion we have reminded our children how important it is to choose the right friends because *"the companion of fools suffers harm."* (Proverbs 14:20 NIV).

Develop a personal campaign for your life or your child's life with one particular powerful verse. One evening our five-year-old son came downstairs after bedtime to tell his dad he couldn't sleep. Fortunately, rather than acting on his first reflex, which was to shout, "Get back to bed!", my husband asked Lloyd what was keeping him awake. Lloyd opened up to David about his fears of the dark, fears of the unknown. David gently reminded Lloyd of a verse he had learned in song, *"When I am afraid, I will trust in You,"* (Psalms 56:3). They talked about God's love for Lloyd and how the Bible taught us to turn to God and trust Him when we were afraid. They sang the song together as David tucked Lloyd back into bed, and ended their evening with that same thought for the next several bedtimes. Lloyd learned several valuable lessons from that opportunity:

- he learned that God cares for us,
- that the answers to life's problems can be found in the Bible,
- that the Bible is an excellent resource in a time of need,
- that God's Word can be of great help after we've stored it in our brains, and finally,
- that his Dad is a man who turns to God for answers to life's problems.

Use the verses you learn to bless those you know outside your family. Incorporate Biblical references into your daily conversations, make your walk with God a something that you share with others. Making a brief quote from a verse as part of a discussion in your daily interactions with others or in a written correspondence lets them know the value you place on Scripture and thus your relationship with God, and may encourage them to seek a stronger relationship with God. Having Scripture be part of your walking, talking testimony flows when the words are "hidden in your heart", and gives your discussions a more natural feel that's not likely to happen if you have to whip out your Bible and flip through it to look for the words!

One morning as my husband walked our kindergartener Lloyd to the bus stop, they were having a discussion about one of the verses they had listened to while eating breakfast, *"Therefore, as God's chosen people, holy and dearly loved, clothe yourselves with compassion, kindness, humility, gentleness and patience. (Col. 3:12 NIV)."* David reminded Lloyd that "clothe yourselves" meant that when we take on the traits that God wants us to have, these characteristics are what can protect us from the world, and they are the "clothes" that people remember us as having worn. Imagine the joy in David's heart the very next day when he had a call from Lloyd's teacher, just to say what a pleasure she had in being able to teach him. His teacher specifically mentioned that Lloyd was "kind and compassionate". After catching his surprised breath, David thanked the teacher, and then decided to share with her the significance of that phrase in Lloyd's life. He told her that at home they were teaching Lloyd that God told us we should clothe ourselves in "compassion, kindness, humility, gentleness and patience." She assured David that she could sense how well Lloyd was being taught at home. How much more special Lloyd must have seemed to his teacher knowing what instruction he was receiving at home. And hopefully, she was somehow encouraged to grow in her relationship with God.

Most importantly, bring glory to God with your knowledge of the Bible. Use the verses to give you strength in times of temptation as Jesus did in the wilderness, or in times of despair as Jesus did on the cross. Use the verses you learn as prayer in praise to God, who "inhabits our praise" (*But thou art holy, O thou that inhabitest the praises of Israel,* Psalms 22:3, KJV). Imagine what joy it must bring God when He knows that we pursue Him by knowing His word and praising Him with His word.

Don't worry — God doesn't just speak in King James! Find the version YOU can relate to and use it, but there is no law against mixing and matching. Because one school teaches exclusively in KJV, Janet's kids memorize out of that version. I verily admire how they can keep their tongues-eth from being tied-est in knots. Our church tends to use NIV, so most of our verses are memorized from that version. Still, for some, I just like the "oldies but goodies" — especially for the Lord's Prayer or Psalm 23 or the

Christmas story (because that's what Sally quoted in Charlie Brown's Christmas) — but sometimes I can "relate" better to the words as communicated through more contemporary versions.

So, beyond the distinct promise of God that He has promised will NOT return void, does all this effort matter? Does it make a difference? Has it impacted our children and those nieces and nephews we hoped to inspire? Will children retain the verses they've learned? Will those verses serve them in times of need?

Our niece, Katie, had not even been born when we started challenging our family to learn verses. Now she has graduated out of the memory contest and is an adult. She said an amazing 174 verses the year she was 18 while a busy freshman in college. Here's what she wrote, unsolicited, after her last Christmas saying memory verses:

> *"I seriously appreciate all that you have given to me over the years. It, in itself, has created a ministry and straight mind for us grandkids who store the Word of God in us, and I thank both of you for the consistent encouragement."*

And what about Jennifer, the niece who started it all, the one who said verses each Christmas from the year she was nine until she reached adulthood at 18? Over that time she said an amazing total of 731 verses. A few years later she sent us a card, which said:

> *"Dear Aunt Kenya and Uncle David,*
> *I want to thank you for the annual memory verse 'contest'… This past July*

when I hit my head playing roller-hockey was one of those times that I was extremely grateful that I had 'hidden (His) word in my heart.' In the ER, I was initially scared because of the extreme pain and dizziness...It was at that time that many of the verses I have memorized over the years came into my mind. Thank you for the extra encouragement to learn Scripture... Jen"

She recovered from her fall. She and her husband, Andrew, are now proud parents of two-year-old twins, and we recently received a video from them showing the twins learning their first Bible verses...hiding His word in their hearts. Happy Hiding!

And walk in love, just as Christ also loved you,
and gave Himself up for us, an offering and a sacrifice to God as a fragrant aroma.

―――

Ephesians 5:2 NASB

**Do not swerve
to the right
or the left;
keep your foot
from evil.**

Proverbs 4:27

Walk in all the way
that the LORD your God has
commanded you,
so that you may
live and prosper
and prolong your days
in the land
that you will possess.

———

Deuteronomy 5:33

My dear brothers,
take note of this.
Everyone should be
quick to listen,
slow to speak and
slow to become angry.

———
James 1:19

Remain in me, and I will
remain in you. No branch can
bear fruit by itself;
it must remain in the vine.
Neither can you bear fruit
unless you remain in me.

John 15:4

**For the wages
of sin is death,
but the gift of God
is eternal life
in Christ Jesus
our Lord.**

―――
Romans 6:23

As the deer pants for
streams of water,
so my soul pants
for you, O God.

Psalm 42:1

Jesus replied,
"Love the Lord
your God
with all you heart and with all
your soul and with all your
mind."

Matthew 22:37

**Turn from evil
and do good;
seek peace
and pursuit it.**

Psalm 34:14

Carry each other's burdens,
and in this way
you will fulfill
the law of Christ.

Galatians 6:2

WRONG WAY

There is a way
that seems right
to a man,
but in the end
it leads to death.

———

Proverbs 14:12

Jesus answered,
"I am the way
and the truth
and the life.
No one comes
to the Father
except
through me."

John 14:6

**He must
become greater;
I must
become less.**

———

John 3:30

Heaven and earth will pass away,
but my words
will never
pass away.

Luke 21:33

**For as high as
the heavens are
above the earth,
so great is His love
for those who fear Him.**

Psalm 103:11

**Whatever you do, work at it
with all your heart,
as working
for the Lord,
not for men.**

———

Colossians 3:23

**The house
of the wicked
will be destroyed,
but the tent of the upright
will flourish.**

Proverbs 14:11

No temptation has seized you except what is common to man. And God is faithful; he will not let you be tempted beyond what you can bear. But when you are tempted, he will also provide a way out so that you can stand up under it.

1 Corinthians 10:13

THRU TRAFFIC

No, in all
these things
we are more
than conquerors through him
who loved us.

———
Romans 8:37

Train up a child
in the way
he should go,
and when he is old
he will not turn
from it.

———

Proverbs 22:6

Trust in the LORD
with all your heart
and lean not on
your own understanding.

———

Proverbs 3:5

I tell you the truth,
anyone who will not receive
the kingdom of God
like a little child
will never enter it.

―――――
Mark 10:15

Do not be anxious
about anything,
but in everything,
by prayer and petition,
with thanksgiving,
present your requests to God.

———

Philippians 4:6

Since, then, you have been raised with Christ, set your hearts on things above, where Christ is seated at the right hand of God. Set your minds on things above, not on earthly things.

Colossians 3:1,2

I have been crucified with
Christ and I no longer live,
but Christ lives in me.
The life I live in the body,
I live by faith
in the Son of God,
who loved me and gave
himself for me.

Galatians 2:20

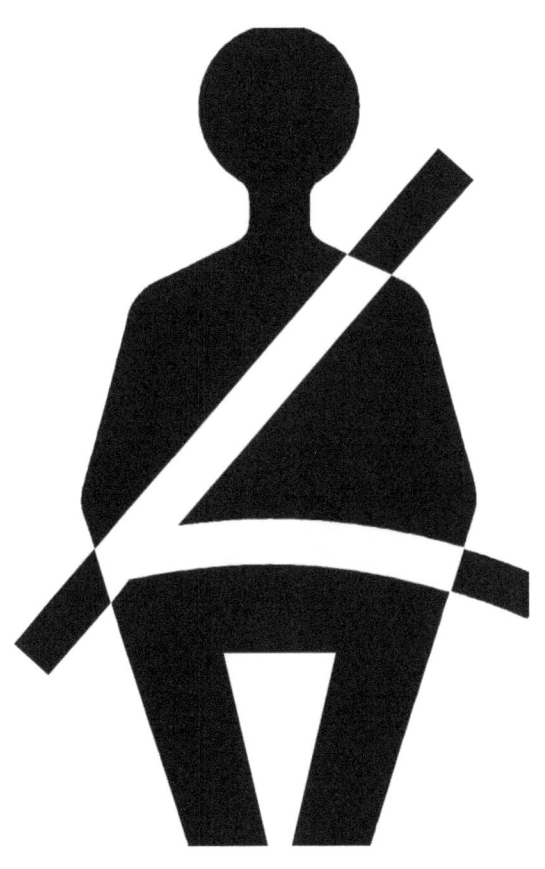

Stand firm then, with the belt
of truth buckled
around your waist, with the
breastplate of righteousness
in place...

———
Ephesians 6:14

A gentle answer
turns away wrath,
but a harsh word
stirs up anger.

Proverbs 15:1

**He who dwells
in the shelter
of the Most High
will rest in the shadow
of the Almighty.**

Psalm 91:1

So be careful
to do what
the LORD your God has
commanded you;
do not turn aside
to the right
or to the left.

———

Deuteronomy 5:32

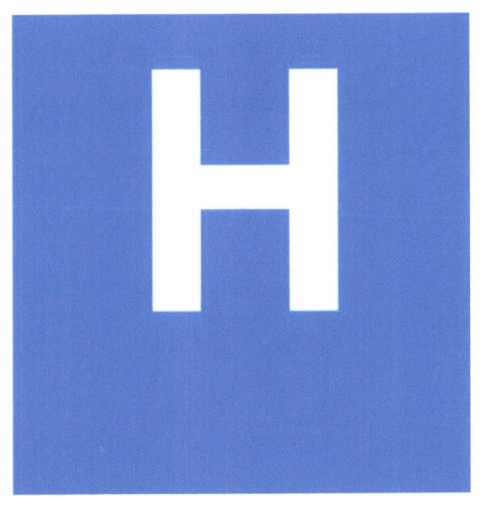

And the God of all grace,
who called you
to his eternal glory in Christ,
after you have suffered
a little while,
will himself restore you and
make you strong,
firm and steadfast.

---

1 Peter 5:10

No discipline seems pleasant
at the time,
but painful.
Later on, however,
it produces a harvest of
righteousness
and peace
for those who have been
trained by it.

Hebrews 12:11

**Call to me
and I will answer you
and tell you great and
unsearchable things
you do not know.**

Jeremiah 33:3

But he said to me,
"My grace is
sufficient for you,
for my power is made
perfect in weakness."
Therefore I will boast
all the more gladly
about my weaknesses,
so that Christ's power
may rest on me.

———

2 Corinthians 12:9

**In addition to all this,
take up the shield of faith,
with which you can extinguish
all the flaming arrows
of the evil one.**

Ephesians 6:16

**FOOD · PHONE
GAS · LODGING
HOSPITAL
CAMPING
SECOND RIGHT**

And my God
will meet
all your needs
according to his glorious
riches
in Christ Jesus.

———

Philippians 4:19

Remember Lot's wife!

Luke 17:32

RIGHT LANE MUST TURN RIGHT

Likewise every good tree
bears good fruit,
but a bad tree
bears bad fruit.

Matthew 7:17

I have hidden
your word in my heart
that I might not
sin against you.

―――
Psalm 119:11

We live by faith not by sight.

―――

2 Corinthians 5:7

Now we see but a poor
reflection as in a mirror;
then we shall see face to face.
Now I know in part; then I
shall know fully,
even as I am fully known.

———
1 Corinthians 13:12

DIVIDED HIGHWAY ENDS

For this reason a man will
leave his father and mother
and be united to his wife, and
the two will become one flesh.

Matthew 19:5

About the Author

Kenya Anders is a dermatologist who lives in Peachtree City, Georgia. She and her husband, David, have five children: Rebekah, Lloyd, Luke, Rachel and Lincoln.

David Anders Publishing House — a Writer's Studio® was established to provide new authors assistance with access to the world of professional publication. As a publisher of quality writings we hope to be adding continuously to our studio of writers and the list of their fine works.

If you have a friend who is trying to get a book published, tell him or her about us — or maybe you are ready to take that step yourself. Visit our website and bookstore at www.AndersUSA.com.

Books we are proud to be featuring currently include:

20/80 A Love Letter…Sort Of
by David L. Anders

This fictional romantic comedy is a story of humor, romance, wisdom and foolishness. David Patson is a Pre-Med student at the University of Georgia who awakens carefree on his 20th birthday, May 25, 1977, then meets three uninvited strangers who crash his party and take him on what can only be described as the journey of a lifetime.

Octogenarians Say the Darndest Things
by David L. Anders with Rebekah Yates Anders

Life doesn't begin at 80, but it doesn't have to end there either. This mother-son team of physicians with over 75 years of patient care experience recalls the humor, wisdom, pathos and surprises revealed while caring for this remarkable group of people.

The Silver Bell
by Rebekah Yates Anders
with illustrations by Rachel Elizabeth Anders

In this short story for children and adults, a young boy demonstrates caring and another view of the love of Christmas is revealed.

You Might Be a Problem Drinker If…
by David L. Anders

Hilarious and yet insightful, more than 100 ways to know if maybe it's time to cut down on the drinking (or increase your life insurance coverage!).

You Might Be a Problem Drinker If… Let's Have Another Round!
by David L. Anders

Picking up where he left off with the first volume in this series, the author provides more than 100 subtle or not so subtle signs that alcohol is causing problems for you or those who nag you.

www.ingramcontent.com/pod-product-compliance
Lightning Source LLC
Chambersburg PA
CBHW041522090426
42737CB00037B/6